IMAGES
of America

K&B
DRUG STORES

ON THE COVER: A fountain attendant waits on customers wanting curb fountain services outside Katz & Besthoff no. 5 at 7133 St. Charles Avenue. From the look of the automobile parked outside, this photograph dates to the late 1930s. According to Sydney Besthoff III, curb service did not last much longer after this time.

IMAGES
of America

K&B
DRUG STORES

John S. Epstein
Foreword by Sydney J. Besthoff III

ARCADIA
PUBLISHING

Published by Arcadia Publishing
Charleston, South Carolina

Printed in the United States of America

Library of Congress Control Number: 2010939832

For all general information, please contact Arcadia Publishing:
Telephone 843-853-2070
Fax 843-853-0044
E-mail sales@arcadiapublishing.com
For customer service and orders:
Toll-Free 1-888-313-2665

Visit us on the Internet at www.arcadiapublishing.com

To Judith, this is the drug store that I grew up with and loved.

CONTENTS

ACKNOWLEDGMENTS

This project began a few years ago when I was trying to direct someone to the nearest drug store and inadvertently directed them to the K&B on the next corner. The problem with my directions was that K&B drug store had been sold to Rite Aid several years earlier and was no longer in business, except in my mind. The person I had given the directions to asked what a K&B was, and it occurred to me that there was no fast answer to that question. Because K&B was more than a drug store—it was a part of my childhood and a part of New Orleans that is forever tied to its history. With that in mind, I wanted to remember this wonderful piece of New Orleans history I have been privileged to grow up with and enjoy.

First, let me thank Sydney Besthoff III for answering my blind letter, which asked if he would grant me his blessings to write a short book about K&B drug stores. I was delighted to receive a reply two days later, personally inviting me to his office to see his scrapbooks and memorabilia. The letter he wrote was even signed in purple ink—K&B purple ink. Many years ago, I read a description of a gentleman who was described as a "merchant prince." I never really understood the meaning of the phrase until I met Sydney Besthoff III. He defines it.

I also would like to thank Mr. Besthoff's personal assistant, Pamela Shaw, who helped me scan photographs and answered all of my countless questions. She was never too busy to answer my e-mails or phone calls and, like Mr. Besthoff, was always helpful in identifying people and locations in photographs. This entire experience would not have been possible without her invaluable help. I truly appreciate it.

My wife, Michelle, and daughter Judith deserve thanks for listening about K&B drug stores over the past year on an hourly basis. Both always encouraged me and made the project fun from the beginning.

Also, thanks certainly goes to Amy Perryman, acquisitions editor for Arcadia Publishing, for her support from the beginning. I would never have been able to complete this book without her guidance.

Finally, I would like to thank Sydney Besthoff Sr. and Gustave Katz for opening a drug store in 1905 that has touched so many lives, including mine. What a great place. I'll never forget it.

FOREWORD

Katz and Besthoff (K&B) is as much a part of New Orleans history as jazz, Mardi Gras, street cars, the French Quarter, and beignets.

If you are 20-plus years old, K&B is a treasured memory that is a part of each of us. Everyone relates to the memory of K&B in their own specific way—the K&B Ice Cream, the K&B Beer, or, if you are older, the soda fountain located inside K&B and the pleasure of enjoying a Nectar Soda while shopping. Most profoundly recognized was the "K&B Purple," which, even today, is considered any color of purple closely resembling the color of the K&B logo and private label items throughout the stores.

More than a decade has passed since the closing of K&B Drug stores, but the cultural significance lives on with a great following of nostalgists.

While many of these memories will never be again, photographs and captions help us remember and show young ones the way things were when K&B was around.

As many with memories of K&B, John Epstein has a passion for those recollections—so much so to have taken the time and efforts to share with all. Enjoy!

—Sydney Besthoff III, October 2010

INTRODUCTION

K&B, as it was officially known when it was sold to Rite Aid, was far from the small neighborhood drug store started by Gustave Katz of New Orleans and Sydney Besthoff of Memphis in 1905. Although a multistate chain at its sale in 1997, K&B was always true to its commitment of "Only the Best," the drug store's original slogan when it opened. The drug stores were known as Katz & Besthoff (although the Katz family had sold their interests to the Besthoffs after Katz's death in 1940), until the name officially changed in 1977 to K&B. Sydney Besthoff III has documented the story of K&B's growth from the day it opened until the last issue of the *K&B Connection*, the official K&B newsletter, in 1997. The scrapbooks are filled with photographs of various stores as they opened during the lifetime of the company.

In the early days of K&B, another merchant's refusal of purple wrapping paper used to protect purchased goods was acquired at a discount by Katz & Besthoff, resulting in the shade of purple that has become the K&B trademark. A slogan derived from the use of the purple paper was, "If it's purple on the outside, it's Only the Best from Katz & Besthoff." From one small seemingly insignificant location at 732 Canal Street to the close of K&B in 1997, there were 50 locations in New Orleans and 135 other locations spread over six states, including Louisiana. All of the stores reflected what Sydney Besthoff Sr. and Gustave Katz envisioned—drug stores committed to good prices, quality, quantity, and outstanding service.

Katz & Besthoff started off slowly, opening only four stores in their first 18 years of business. There were neither suburbs nor malls; Canal Street, St. Charles, Carrollton, Claiborne and Napoleon Avenues comprised the shopping areas of the city. Many of the Katz & Besthoff original locations are now under the Rite Aid name and are still in business at these same locations. The drug stores could usually be found on a corner, covering two streets instead of one. All had curb and delivery service for their customers at one time, and all were K&B purple. The curb service "didn't last too long," according to Sydney Besthoff III. A photograph of one of the early locations shows a sign out front reading, "no curb service, please come in." Apparently, the curb service had kept people out of the drug store, causing a loss in profits. The delivery service lasted until the late 1950s, and each location had a bicycle delivery person and a truck to deliver items.

As the years went by, liability issues made the bicycle delivery service unfeasible and, eventually, truck delivery service suffered the same fate. As the business grew, Katz & Besthoff changed with the times, updating locations when business demanded more modern facilities. In 1926, Sydney Besthoff Sr. died and his son Sydney Besthoff Jr., a registered pharmacist, entered the business. In 1965, Sydney Besthoff III was named executive vice president of the company, and for the next 30 years, the drug store experienced exponential growth. Sydney Besthoff Jr. retired in 1972 and died in 1982. In 1987, Sydney Besthoff III named James LeBlanc, who started with K&B as a pharmacist in 1957, president and CEO. LeBlanc understood that K&B had to adapt to the ever-changing consumer landscape, and under his and Sydney Besthoff's control, the drug store grew to the multistate operation that was sold to Rite Aid in 1997. At the time of the sale, K&B drug stores employed over 4,800 employees, the majority of whom stayed with the new owner. The drug store business had changed greatly from the time Sydney Besthoff III took it over in the early 1960s and was moving in a direction that wasn't what customers would have expected from their K&B drug stores. When asked about the sale years later, Sydney Besthoff III said quietly, "It was time."

One

THE EARLY YEARS

A photograph of the first Katz & Besthoff drug store, located at 732 Canal Street, shows a typical business of that era, giving no hint of its phenomenal growth over the next 90 years. To a great degree, its success can be linked to the unique inventory and exclusive products, as well as the myriad of services that were offered, including photographic processing. Exclusive products from the cosmetics counter were proudly embossed with "Katz & Besthoff, New Orleans," adding little doubt to their origin.

According to advertisements inside the pharmacy, other services available were eye exams, glasses, and cameras from a crowded display case set prominently in the front of the store. There were also several different candy lines, some with the K&B brand as the sole agent. The K&B soda fountains served ice cream that was made fresh daily on the premises to meet customer demand. Delivery service of ice cream was available; the ice cream was made about an hour before the shopper requested it and brought to their home, packed in ice to keep it frozen for customer convenience. From this initial shop, Katz & Besthoff opened four more stores in the next 18 years, most of them within a few miles of the original location. In 1938, under the management of Bill Leeper, K&B opened its own film-processing lab at 1011 Canal Street. With the increasing number of locations and soda fountains, K&B also opened its first ice cream factory facility on Bienville Street around 1928.

Sydney Besthoff Sr., a pharmacist with Besthoff's pharmacy in Memphis, Tennessee, opened the first Katz & Besthoff drug store at 732 Canal Street in the New Orleans downtown shopping district with pharmacist Gustave Katz. Besthoff died in 1926 of a heart attack. (Courtesy Besthoff Family Collection.)

Besthoff's cousins Jac (left) and Charles Stich, who were instrumental in running K&B during the years of World War II, are seen here standing in front of K&B's ice cream manufacturing facility on Bienville Street sometime around the 1940s. (Courtesy Besthoff Family Collection.)

Gustave Katz was a New Orleans pharmacist who owned a drug store on St. Charles and Jackson Avenues before he and pharmacist Sydney Besthoff Sr. opened the Katz & Besthoff drug store on Canal Street. Katz died in 1940, and his family sold their interests in the business to the Besthoff family. (Courtesy Besthoff Family Collection.)

This is a receipt from Gustave Katz's pharmacy on St. Charles and Jackson Avenues in New Orleans. Katz was in business for himself from 1896 to 1905 before partnering with Besthoff. (Courtesy Besthoff Family Collection.)

Seen here is Katz & Besthoff drug store's first location at 732 Canal Street. The drug store only occupied the bottom floor, described by a customer as "20 feet wide and filled with all sizes of jars and ointments." The second and third floors were leased out in the beginning, but eventually became the drug store's home offices after a few years. Note the Huyler's Candy banner across the front window listing Katz & Besthoff as the sole agents to sell their candy. One of the things that made K&B successful was the unique and exclusive items carried in their drug stores. (Courtesy Besthoff Family Collection.)

KATZ & BESTHOFF, INC. DRUGGIST, NEW ORLEANS, LA. MAIN STORE.

This postcard is from the National Show Case Co. and exhibits the display cases at Katz & Besthoff drug store at 732 Canal Street. Customers were assisted by clerks until self service became the norm in drug stores around 1940. Below is the reverse of the postcard. It states that Besthoff is partial to "National" fixtures and has three contracts with the company. This would have been from before 1923, before the fourth K&B location was opened on Carrollton and Oak Streets. (Both author's collection.)

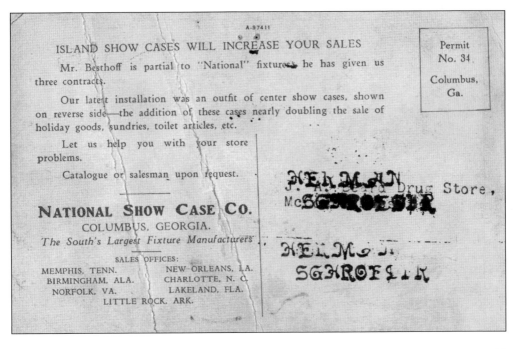

A-97411

ISLAND SHOW CASES WILL INCREASE YOUR SALES

Mr. Besthoff is partial to "National" fixtures he has given us three contracts.

Our latest installation was an outfit of center show cases, shown on reverse side—the addition of these cases nearly doubling the sale of holiday goods, sundries, toilet articles, etc.

Let us help you with your store problems.

Catalogue or salesman upon request.

NATIONAL SHOW CASE CO.

COLUMBUS, GEORGIA.

The South's Largest Fixture Manufacturers

SALES OFFICES:

MEMPHIS, TENN.   NEW ORLEANS, LA.
BIRMINGHAM, ALA.   CHARLOTTE, N. C.
NORFOLK, VA.   LAKELAND, FLA.
LITTLE ROCK, ARK.

Permit No. 34

Columbus, Ga.

HERMAN Drug Store,
McSCHROEDER

HELMA J.
SGHROESER

This early photograph of 732 Canal Street illustrates the drug store's changes from its early days with the enlargement of the storefront. The window (left) is filled with thermoses on sale. S.J.Besthoff Jr. captured this image in 1916. (Courtesy Besthoff Family Collection.)

Seen here are display cabinets at the 732 Canal Street drug store. Russell McPhail Candy fills the counters. Katz & Besthoff carried exclusive products, which set their drug store apart from other ones in the city. (Courtesy Besthoff Family Collection.)

This photograph shows the front display area that could be seen upon entering the Katz & Besthoff at 732 Canal Street. On display are cameras, cosmetics, toys, and candy. Signs above the display cabinet advertise optical services and eyeglasses. Note that the optical sign advertises the services of a female optometrist; there were only a few in the United States at that time. (Courtesy Besthoff Family Collection.)

Katz & Besthoff's second location at 841 Canal Street opened in 1911. The store was across Dauphine Street from the Maison Blanche department store and near the D.H. Holmes department store. (Courtesy Besthoff Family Collection.)

The soda fountain at Katz & Besthoff drug store's second location at 841 Canal Street opened in 1911. This 1930s photograph shows the fountain decorated for Christmas. Note the seat coverings and ornate light fixtures. (Courtesy Besthoff Family Collection.)

Above is Katz & Besthoff drug store's third location, opened in 1920 in the Ghisalberti building on the corner of St. Charles and Louisiana Avenues. This photograph dates from the mid-1960s, a few months before the building was torn down to build a modern K&B drug store. The new building still stands today as a Rite Aid drug store. (Courtesy Besthoff Family Collection.)

This photograph, taken in the mid-1960s, offers a closer look at the K&B on St. Charles and Louisiana Avenues. Note the old streetlights and the street names tiled into the sidewalks in front. The K&B Drug Store stood on this corner in this building since the 1920s until a new K&B was built on this site in the 1960s. (Courtesy Besthoff Family Collection.)

★ KATZ & BESTHOFF LTD

Druggists

Office 841 Canal . . . . MA gnolia-1231
Ice cream dept 523 Bienville . . . . MA gnolia-1231
Warehouse 523 Bienville . . . . MA gnolia-1231

Stores:

No 1 732 Canal . . . . MA gnolia-1231
No 2 841 Canal . . . . MA gnolia-1231
No 3 3401 St Chas . . . . UP town-1900
No 4 8040 Oak . . . . WA lnut-1111
No 5 7133 St Chas . . . . WA lnut-5700
No 6 Napoleon & S Claiborne . . . . . . UP town-5200
No 7 3120 Canal . . . . GA lvez-4151
No 8 1400 N Broad . . . . GA lvez-1101
No 9 235 Carondelet . . . . RA ymond-0401
No 10 St Chas & Napoleon . . . . UP town-3900
No 11 3940 Canal . . . . GA lvez-1125
No 12 1011 Canal . . . . MA gnolia-5555

FROM 8 PM TO 12 MIDNIGHT ON WEEK
DAYS & FROM 1 PM TO 12 MIDNIGHT
ON SUNDAYS & HOLIDAYS CALL AS
FOLLOWS:

No 1 732 Canal . . . . MA gnolia-5678
No 2 841 Canal . . . . MA gnolia-4754

A 1937 New Orleans telephone directory lists the 12 locations of Katz & Besthoff throughout the area. All the locations were within a few miles of each other. It wasn't until the 1950s that K&B drug stores opened in the surrounding parishes of New Orleans. (Author's collection.)

Katz & Besthoff's fourth location on Oak Street and Carrollton Avenues opened in 1923. The original building was torn down in 1962 and this one replaced it. The building still stands today under the Rite Aid name. (Courtesy Besthoff Family Collection.)

Two

PHARMACY

All K&B pharmacies were pretty similar; nothing set them apart from any other except for the rare occasions when something different was introduced. K&B's introduction of its logo, an oval with two check marks diagonally across from the letters K and B, distinguished it from the other pharmacies around. The logo represented K&B prescriptions being double-checked by pharmacists before they were dispensed to customers. Confirming that the prescriptions were correct was a practice initiated by Gustave Katz, when he owned his own pharmacy on St. Charles and Jackson Avenues. The logo was immediately recognizable to K&B customers and assured them that errors was unlikely as a result of double-checking medications.

Pharmacy shelves were filled to capacity with every imaginable type of medication. There were clerk-assisted cabinets filled with items from floor to ceiling and running from the front to the back of the drug stores. In later years, K&B's pharmacies were stocked with items that most pharmacies should carry but didn't due to cost limitations or lack of space. When customers at a competitor's pharmacy couldn't find an item, they were usually directed to K&B. If K&B pharmacy didn't carry an item, then it probably didn't exist. From observing the old images of the pharmacies through the years, one may find it unbelievable how much inventory was on hand in these local stores. Pharmacies today don't come close to the selection that K&B carried, even in its earliest years.

From the very beginning, Katz & Besthoff was unique; the stores catered to the individual customer with a selection that would rival any large drug store chain. K&B drug stores were the forerunner of drug store models today.

The Katz & Besthoff double-checked logo represented prescriptions being "double checked" by pharmacists before they were dispensed to their customers. This logo was used until the store's name was officially changed to K&B in 1977. (Author's collection.)

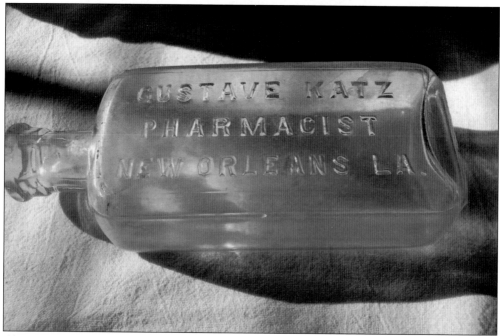

Above is a prescription bottle left over from Gustave Katz's pharmacy at St. Charles and Jackson Avenues in New Orleans. Very few items still exist from Katz's solo venture as a pharmacist in 1896. (Author's collection.)

Each K&B pharmacy had a bicycle delivery person and a delivery truck. In this photograph from the late 1930s, "Junior," the messenger at store no. 14, is ready to deliver prescriptions to customers around New Orleans. According to Sydney Besthoff III, the messenger service was eventually discontinued due to liability issues and costs that outweighed its convenience. (Courtesy Besthoff Family Collection.)

Personalized Pharmacy Services

For your convenience we maintain your personal prescription records via our computerized system. Each prescription is checked for drug interactions and allergy screening.

- ✓ Dedicated, concerned pharmacists
- ✓ Convenient locations
- ✓ Most Third Party Plans accepted
- ✓ Exclusive Pharmacy Computer System
- ✓ Generic equivalent savings
- ✓ Major Credit Cards accepted

...Since 1905

Seen here is another K&B pharmacy with numerous medications filling the shelves. This image was captured at the pharmacy laboratory in the K&B located at 3705 Jefferson Highway. The original typed formulas from Katz and Besthoff still exist, attesting to the accuracy and consistency of their medications. (Courtesy Besthoff Family Collection.)

At left is a pharmacy prescription sheet used during the last few years that K&B was in business. The K&B logo changed after 1977, doing away with the double-checked logo. The sheet was colored purple, K&B's trademark since 1911. (Author's collection.)

Registered pharmacist Sydney Besthoff Jr. joined K&B after his father's death in 1926. He was active in the business over the next 46 years until retirement in 1972. Sydney Besthoff Jr. died in 1982. (Courtesy Besthoff Family Collection.)

Sydney Besthoff Jr. (left) pours medication into a Katz & Besthoff prescription bottle. Standing next to Besthoff is Edward Chapotel, the original manager of store no. 2, which opened in 1911 at 841 Canal Street. This photograph was taken in 1959 when Chapotel was vice president and general manager of Katz & Besthoff drug stores. (Courtesy Besthoff Family Collection.)

This 732 Canal Street Katz & Besthoff window advertises Pharmacy Week, probably during the First World War, according to the design of the window. Window advertising was important in attracting customers who shopped on Canal Street during its heyday. (Courtesy Besthoff Family Collection.)

This photograph was taken at the Katz & Besthoff on St. Charles and Napoleon Avenues sometime during the 1940s. This drug store was demolished in 1955 and rebuilt to modernize the location. (Courtesy Besthoff Family Collection.)

K&B RX News was mailed to customers and provided information about the pharmacy. The article on the front of this issue from March 1956 shows vice president Edward L. Chapotel (left) and president Sydney Besthoff Jr. (center) receiving an award for filling their 10-millionth prescription. (Courtesy Besthoff Family Collection.)

The *K&B RX News* from May 1956 celebrated K&B's 51st year in business. These were mailed out to K&B customers offering them a free quart of ice cream for visiting the pharmacy. (Courtesy Besthoff Family Collection.)

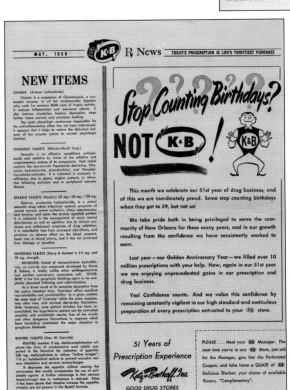

This display offers 12 reasons why doctors should have their prescriptions filled by Katz & Besthoff. This was in 1938, when Katz & Besthoff had four stores and 80 registered pharmacists. (Courtesy Besthoff Family Collection.)

At right, Sydney Besthoff III poses in front of the 1938 display offering 12 reasons why doctors should have their prescriptions filled by Katz & Besthoff. Over the next 60 years, Besthoff III would oversee the drug store's growth to 180 more locations in six states, including Louisiana. New Orleans alone had over 50 locations. (Courtesy Besthoff Family Collection.)

This newly opened K&B pharmacy at the Veterans Highway location in 1970 is filled with merchandise. The lady behind the counter was there to help customers in the friendliest manner possible, as was the rest of K&B's staff. (Courtesy Besthoff Family Collection.)

The pharmacies in the older K&B drug stores were located in the rear of the stores and on an elevated platform. By the 1990s, the newer K&B drug stores put the pharmacies at floor level to make the area more customer friendly. (Courtesy Besthoff Family Collection.)

This photograph, dating from the 1950s, shows the Katz & Besthoff delivery vehicles and drivers assigned to the various K&B locations in the New Orleans area. Each drug store had a uniformed driver on call. (Courtesy Besthoff Family Collection.)

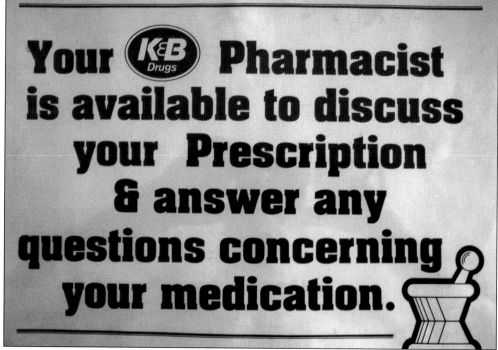

Your **K&B** Pharmacist is available to discuss your Prescription & answer any questions concerning your medication.

These signs were hung in K&B pharmacies inviting customers to ask questions and speak with their pharmacists. A practice commonly done today, it was an innovation pioneered by K&B drug stores. (Author's collection.)

From the early days, K&B pharmacy had delivery vehicles available at each location. In this image, a uniformed driver stands proudly next to his delivery vehicle. K&B had a fleet of these available to accommodate each drug store. (Courtesy Besthoff Family Collection.)

As K&B's locations grew, their fleet of delivery vehicles located at each location multiplied. Naturally, these vehicles were purple. Delivery service was discontinued in the late 1950s. (Courtesy Besthoff Family Collection.)

The photograph seen here was taken from the pharmacist's elevated perspective, looking down at the selection-filled aisles of an unknown K&B location. In the 1990s, the pharmacy sections of all K&B locations added customer consultation areas. (Courtesy Besthoff Family Collection.)

This image was captured around 1970 at the K&B in the Clearview Shopping Center of Metairie, Louisiana, a suburb of New Orleans. Zeas restaurant occupies the location today. (Courtesy Besthoff Family Collection.)

This photograph proves that K&B's pharmacy selection was never in short supply. The shelves are filled with everything from aspirin to ballpoint pens. (Courtesy Besthoff Family Collection.)

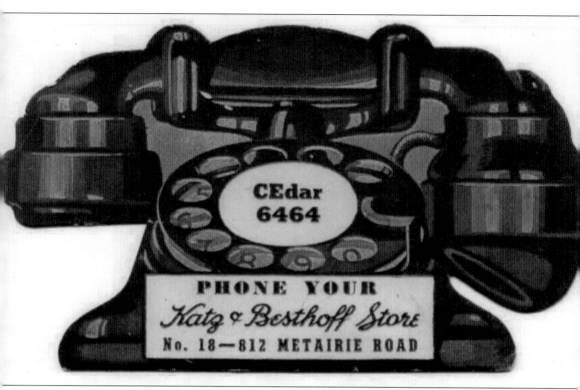

This postcard, which features a purple telephone on the front, was mailed to customers when a new location was opened. This ended up on a customer's refrigerator just like advertising magnets today. (Author's collection.)

Three

SODA FOUNTAIN

The best way to get an accurate picture of the Katz & Besthoff drug store soda fountains, from their early days until their closing in 1977, is to look at some of the old menus that listed the available items and services. For a few years in the beginning, Katz & Besthoff offered curb service from the soda fountain at all locations. A menu from the late 1930s shows that the menu lists a few lunch items while concentrating on sodas and ice cream. Ice cream was made at each location until 1928, and then an ice cream facility was opened on Bienville Street. This facility lasted until 1948, when K&B moved their ice cream plant and offices to 900 Camp Street. Menus from the 1940s advertise home delivery of ice cream in ice-packed containers and also Flat Fifths, a one-fifth gallon of ice cream sold in containers roughly the size of an ice tray.

By the 1970s, the soda fountains were being phased out and were finally closed, with the last one shutting down in 1977 at Clearview Shopping Center in Metairie, Louisiana. After the fountains closed, K&B continued to make and sell ice cream for their drug stores. The ice cream was made at K&B's Labarre Road distribution center, which opened in the 1970s. K&B made over 50 flavors and, according to Sydney Besthoff III, at one time had a "flavor of the week," instituted by one of his daughters when she managed the facility. Besthoff relayed that the flavors were very popular and that his daughter seemed to know what combination of flavors the public would enjoy. "Of course, the flavors were all too sweet for me," Besthoff admitted with a smile. A decade after K&B's closing, many still miss K&B ice cream and, for those a little older, the soda fountains that used to serve it.

Katz & Besthoff's second location at 841 Canal Street opened in 1911. This photograph appears to have been taken in the 1920s during a hot afternoon. New Orleans heat during the summer increased soda fountain sales. (Courtesy Besthoff Family Collection.)

Curb service was available for soda fountain services at all drug store locations up until about 1940. This is the front of a curb service menu from the time. Included on the menu was a small selection of sandwiches and snack items. (Author's collection.)

On the reverse side of the curb service menu is an advertisement for ice cream delivery to homes. Also advertised are Flat Fifths, a one-fifth gallon of ice cream made to fit in the small freezers of the time. (Author's collection.)

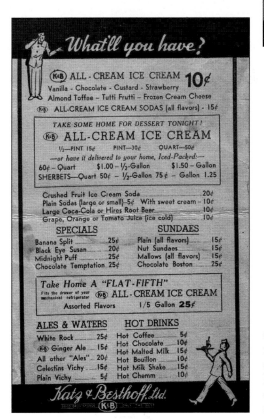

This K&B's freezer is filled with Flat Fifths and ice cream rolls ready to be sold and delivered to customers' homes. The Flat Fifths were popular until larger combined refrigerator and freezer units came about. Flat Fifths were no longer made after the late 1950s. (Courtesy Besthoff Family Collection.)

Home delivery was available from all locations. Ice cream orders in the late 1930s were most likely delivered with this Indian motorcycle. The color of the motorcycle was K&B purple. (Courtesy Besthoff Family Collection.)

This is the K&B soda fountain at the corner of Oak Street and Carrollton Avenue. This was K&B's fourth location, which opened in 1923. This store was rebuilt in 1962 with a larger soda fountain, as seen here. (Courtesy Besthoff Family Collection.)

Even the smaller K&B locations had soda fountains; they were a little more compact. Delivery was available from all locations. (Courtesy Besthoff Family Collection.)

This is the Louisiana and St. Charles Avenue location sometime in the late 1960s before it was torn down. Note the updated fixtures as compared to the fixtures in the photograph taken during the 1920s. K&B updated their stores on a regular basis, keeping up with the interior designs of the times. (Courtesy Besthoff Family Collection.)

This K&B location at St. Charles and Napoleon Avenues had a very small area set aside for soda fountain customers. The store was demolished and rebuilt in 1955. This photograph dates back to around the 1940s. Note the menus at each table; a menu from this location can be seen on the next page. A Capitol One bank now occupies this site. (Courtesy Besthoff Family Collection.)

This is a menu from the K&B at St. Charles and Napoleon Avenues from around the 1940s. The soda fountain menu selections were beginning to include more food items, in addition to the sodas and ice cream. (Author's collection.)

At left is the back of the same menu, offering home delivery and K&B's Flat Fifths, which fit nicely into the small freezer compartments of older refrigerators. (Author's collection.)

K&B Triple Decker Toasted Sandwiches

No. 1 — Chicken Salad and Bacon .... .35
No. 2 — Ham, Swiss Cheese and Lettuce .... .35
No. 3 — Ham, Lettuce and Tomato .... .35
No. 4 — Chicken Salad, Lettuce and Tomato .... .30
No. 5 — Deviled Smithfield Ham and Swiss .
       Cheese .... .35
No. 6 — Imported Sardines, Sliced Egg with
       Lettuce and Tomato .... .35

No. 7 — Club Special .... .45

No. 8 — Tuna Fish Salad and Swiss Cheese .... .30
No. 9 — Egg Salad, Lettuce and Tomato .... .25
No. 10 — Tuna Fish Salad, Lettuce and Tomato .30

With Potato Salad 5c Extra

K&B Salad Bowl WITH DRINK 25¢

Tasty salad on crisp lettuce leaf garnished with
olive, slice of pickle and slice of egg. Served
with crackers and any 5c drink.
WITH CHICKEN SALAD 30c

K&B Super Sandwiches

Made Fresh to Your Order

Bacon and Lettuce .15   Tomato Salad .15
Boiled Ham .... .15   Roast Veal ...... .20
Bacon and Egg .... .20   Egg Salad .... .15
Swiss Cheese ..... .15   Pimiento Cheese . .15
Chicken Salad .... .15   Sliced Chicken .. .30
Minced Ham ...... .15   Bacon and Tomato .20
Ham and Cheese .. .15   Tuna Fish .... .20
Minced Ham & Egg .20   Peanut Butter and
American Cheese .. .15   Jelly .... .15
Imported Sardines .20

With Potato Salad 5c Extra

K&B Cold Luncheon Plate - 25¢

A satisfying lunch including potato chips, meat,
cheese, sardines and salad. Served
with bread and butter.
WITH CHICKEN SALAD 30c

K&B Combination Special

K&B Malted Milk | with any 15c Sandwich .25
     or | with any 20c Sandwich .30
K&B Ice Cream Soda | with any 25c Sandwich .35

K&B All-Cream Ice Cream

10¢ Plate

Seven Delicious Flavors
GENUINE CREOLE CUSTARD

VANILLA   ALMOND TOFFEE   STRAWBERRY
CHOCOLATE   FROZEN CREAM CHEESE   TUTTI-FRUTTI

K&B All-Cream Ice Cream is made in one of the
most modern sanitary Ice-Cream Plants in the
South. The floor and walls are of glass-smooth
terrazzo tile. The latest scientific equipment pas-
teurizes, homogenizes and freezes K&B Ice Cream
without its being touched by human hands.

SLICED CAKE . . . 10c

K&B Ice Cream Sodas

All Flavors **15¢**

Crushed Fruit Ice Cream Soda any flavor .05
Plain Sodas with Sweet Cream .10

K&B Malted Milk

Any Flavor **20¢**

Ovaltine .... .20   Chocolate Vinross .20
Egg Royal .... .25   Any above with Egg .25

K&B Milk Drinks

Sweet Milk .... .05   Milk Shakes ...... .20
Buttermilk .... .05   Frosted Chocolate .20
Flavored Milks .... .10   Iced Coffee ...... .10

K&B Hot Drinks

Coffee .... .05   Malted Milk ...... .15
Hot Soups .... .10   Milk Shake .... .15
Chocolate .... .10   Ovaltine .... .15
Bouillon .... .10   Tea with Cream or Lemon .05

K&B Sundaes

All Flavors **15¢**

Nut Sundaes ...... .15   Mallows .... .15
Chocolate Cold Fudge .15

K&B Specials

PARFAIT (all flavors) .... .20
Syrup, Ice Cream, Whipped Cream and
a Cherry

MALLOW DREAM .... .25
Strawberry and Vanilla Ice Cream, Nectar
Syrup, Mallow, Nuts, Whipped Cream and
a Cherry

COLD CHOCOLATE. K&B .... .25
Chocolate Syrup mixed with Whipped
Cream, topped with Chocolate Ice Cream
and Whipped Cream

CHOCOLATE BOSTON .... .25
Chocolate Ice Cream, Crushed Pineapple,
Chocolate Sauce, Whipped Cream and a
Cherry

LOLLY POP .... .20
Pineapple and Strawberry Crushed Fruit,
Strawberry and Vanilla Ice Cream,
Whipped Cream and a Cherry

BANANA SPLIT .... .25
Vanilla, Chocolate and Strawberry Ice
Cream on Sliced Banana with Pineapple
and Strawberry Crushed Fruit, Whipped
Cream, Nuts and Cherries

America's Most Delicious Drink
NECTAR
ICE CREAM SODA - - - - - - 15c

K&B Ades 15¢

GRAPE, PINEAPPLE, ORANGE,
LEMON OR LIME
Served with Pineapple and
Orange Sherbet

Fruit Juices

Grape   Orange   Grape Fruit
      Pineapple   Tomato

Served Ice Cold **10¢** Glass

Fresh Fruit

ORANGE and PINEAPPLE SHERBETS
10¢

Ales and Waters

K&B Ginger Ale, Lime Rickey,
   Sparkling Water or Celery Tonic .15
All Other "Ales" .... .20
Celestins Vichy .... .15
Plain Vichy .... .15
White Rock .... .15

Seen here is the inside of the menu pictured on the previous page. The selections for lunch were slowly increasing, but the ice cream items were still the main attraction. Note the Nectar Soda for 15¢. By the 1960s, the menu included more breakfast and lunch items and fewer fountain selections. (Author's collection.)

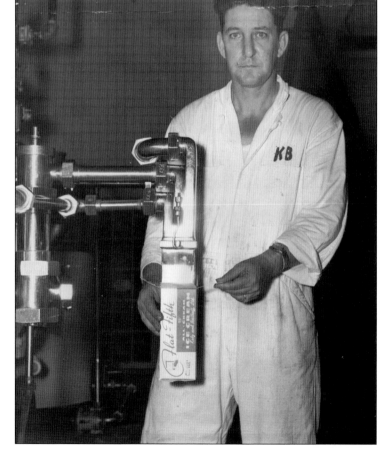

This ice cream facility at 900 Camp Street in New Orleans is where K&B supplied its drug stores and some local restaurants. Pictured is Max Pertuit, plant manager, making a Flat Fifth. (Courtesy Besthoff Family Collection.)

The 900 Camp Street location housed K&B corporate offices, a cafeteria, and the ice cream facility that supplied all K&B locations and some local restaurants with ice cream. The building today houses the Contemporary Arts Center (CAC) of New Orleans. (Courtesy Besthoff Family Collection.)

This Katz & Besthoff delivery truck was used to supply freshly made ice cream to K&B locations around town. K&B also sold and delivered ice cream to some of New Orleans's larger restaurants. K&B's ice cream remained a favorite of its customers, even after the chain's closing in 1997. (Courtesy Besthoff Family Collection.)

In the photograph above, an ice cream roll is being made at K&B's Camp Street facility by an unknown worker. The 900 Camp Street facility supplied ice cream and ice cream novelties to all of the K&B drug stores. (Courtesy Besthoff Family Collection.)

Washington Avenue's Katz & Besthoff soda fountain opened in 1947. The soda fountains were a large part of summertime business, as customers enjoyed good health during the warmer seasons and did not need the pharmacy as much as during the winter. The freezer in the foreground is filled with Flat Fifths and ice cream rolls. (Courtesy Besthoff Family Collection.)

In this 1966 image, a lone customer sits at the K&B soda fountain on St. Charles and Louisiana Avenues. The bicycle out front probably belonged to the delivery person available at this location for customer convenience. In 1967, this building was torn down and a new K&B drug store was built on the site. (Courtesy Besthoff Family Collection.)

This is a K&B logo-enameled glass used to serve Nectar ice cream sodas. The glasses, silverware, and dishes were all adorned with the K&B double-checked logo. During the later years, unmarked glassware and silverware were used. (Author's collection.)

K&B-marked silverware was also used at the soda fountain, along with marked glassware and china. In the last years of K&B's soda fountain operations, the marked china and silverware were discontinued. (Author's collection.)

Early china used at the K&B soda fountain displayed the K&B slogan "Only the Best," which was seen on delivery vehicles and anything else having to do with K&B. Early photographs of the soda fountain on 841 Canal Street show stacks of these dishes used for ice cream and snacks. (Author's collection.)

Later, in the 1960s, china used at K&B soda fountains displayed only the letters K&B. This china was not used very long at the soda fountain. Unmarked glasses and silverware were eventually used at the fountains. (Author's collection.)

This photograph of the Katz & Besthoff drug store at 841 Canal Street was taken around the 1930s or early 1940s. Two soda fountain attendants wait for customers, while other patrons peruse the various counters in the drug store. (Courtesy Besthoff Family Collection.)

This view of K&B's Louisiana and St. Charles Avenues location shows the new soda fountain after its restoration in 1967. Note the sign on the counter that reads, "Mr. K&B says Only the Best." (Courtesy Besthoff Family Collection.)

Even the smallest K&B locations managed to designate an area for a soda fountain; it was an oasis in a busy world. (Courtesy Besthoff Family Collection.)

At left is a food and fountain menu from 1974, one of the last years soda fountains were located in K&B drug stores. (Courtesy Besthoff Family Collection.)

Contents of the 1974 fountain menu show how selections over the years had become less about fountain items and more about food service. The king platter was a favorite with customers, as was the Nectar soda. (Courtesy Besthoff Family Collection.)

Seen here is a 1975 breakfast menu from K&B's soda fountain. The soda fountains only lasted two more years, closing for good in 1977. (Courtesy Besthoff Family Collection.)

By 1975, the menu selections were getting smaller but still provided an adequate breakfast selection. By this time, K&B was ready to start phasing out food service in the drug stores. (Courtesy Besthoff Family Collection.)

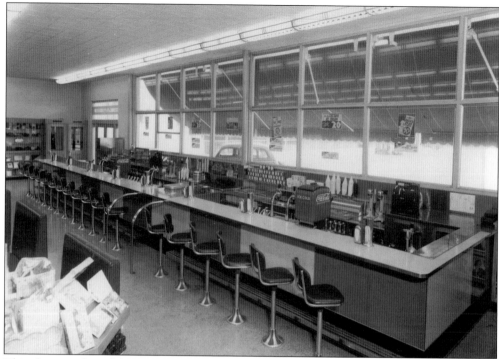

This photograph is of the K&B soda fountain at the Oak Street and Carrollton Avenue location after the drug store was rebuilt in 1962. The soda fountains were taken out of all K&B drug stores in 1977. (Courtesy Besthoff Family Collection.)

The 5225 Canal Boulevard location of K&B reflects the absence of the soda fountain at the newer drug stores. The word "soda" had been completely eliminated from the front. The growth of fast food restaurants had made the drug store fountains obsolete. (Courtesy Besthoff Family Collection.)

Four

PHOTOGRAPHIC
PROCESSING

From the beginning of Katz & Besthoff drug stores, photography and photographic processing, along with cosmetics, the pharmacy, and ice cream, were important part of its business. Stacks of cameras and film boxes of Agfa Plenachrome Film fill the display cases in images of the 732 Canal Street location from 1910, when photography was in its infancy. In 1938, K&B created its own in-house film developing lab at its 1011 Canal Street store, later moving it to its 841 Canal Street location on the third floor. In the beginning, there was only black and white film—color had not yet been produced for the mass market. At most of the K&B locations seen in old photographs, there was advertising in the window or on the side of the building for K&B's film developing service.

The K&B developing process was called Bestone, using the first four letters of the Besthoff name. Naturally, like everything else, the photograph envelopes were K&B purple. As photographic processing got more sophisticated, the envelopes for the pictures got more elaborate, but they always carried the double-checked K&B purple logo. In the late 1970s, when Katz & Besthoff officially became K&B, the logo was changed to reflect a more modern image. Film developing routinely took one day—a courier picked up film from the different K&B locations and returned them to the locations within 24 hours. As the drug stores opened out-of-state locations, the turnaround time was a little longer, but photographs were usually developed within two days. Some, but not all, locations in the last few years had one-hour developing facilities, as well as access to two photographic processing labs owned by K&B drug stores.

The original Katz & Besthoff Camera Center was at the 1011 Canal Street store that opened in 1938. The developing process was known as Bestone, allowing for photographs to be developed in one day. Both sides of the film envelope are shown here. The reverse, below, lists the film speeds for different brands of film popular in the late 1930s. (Both courtesy Besthoff Family Collection.)

VALUABLE FILM INFORMATION

Katz & Besthoff's
CAMERA CENTER
COMPARATIVE FILM SPEED RATINGS

Weston	American Schiener	Din	Weston	American Schiener	Din
6	17	10/10	40	25	18/10
8	18	11/10	50	26	19/10
10	19	12/10	64	27	20/10
12	20	13/10	80	28	21/10
16	21	14/10	100	29	22/10
20	22	15/10	125	30	23/10
24	23	16/10	160	31	24/10
32	24	17/10	200	32	25/10

AVERAGE WESTON RATINGS
Of Frequently Used Film as Given by Weston

	Daylight	Tungsten
Verichrome	50	24
Panatomic X	24	16
Super XX	100	64
Plenachrome	24	16
Superpan Supreme	50	32
Superpan Press	100	64

EASTMAN MOVIE FILM

	Daylight	Tungsten
8mm Pan	8	5
8mm Super X	24	20
16mm Super X	32	24
16mm Super XX	100	64
Kodachrome	8	12

This photograph from the late 1930s was taken at the K&B Camera Center when it was located at 1011 Canal Street. The large selection was later dwarfed when the center moved to the 841 Canal Street location in 1957. (Courtesy Besthoff Family Collection.)

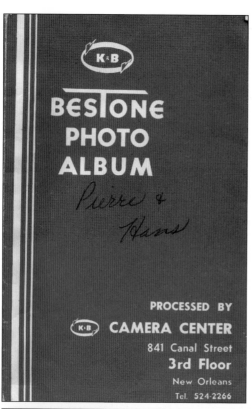

This purple envelope held photographs developed at the Katz & Besthoff Camera Center located on the third floor of the drug store at 841 Canal Street. (Author's collection.)

Below is a K&B Camera Center purple envelope stating that the prints and negatives have been "double checked" for clearness, tone, and detail by K&B experts. (Author's collection.)

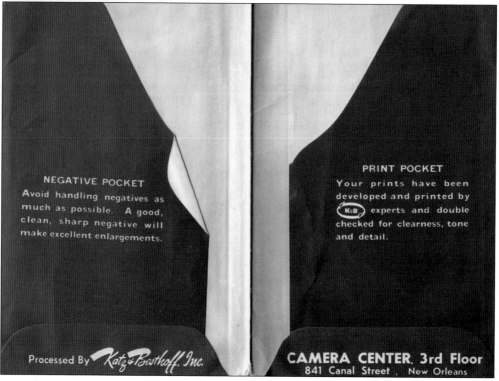

This 1960s photograph shows the remodeled Camera Center on the third floor of 841 Canal Street. In addition to photographic processing, K&B offered a large selection of movie projectors and cameras. In 1978, the Camera Center moved to 227 Dauphine Street. It finally closed in 1995. (Courtesy Besthoff Family Collection.)

This photograph of the K&B Camera Center located on the 3rd floor of K&B at 841 Canal Street shows the modern design of the 1960s and the huge selection of photography items available to customers. (Courtesy Besthoff Family Collection.)

Above is a K&B Camera Center envelope with the old K&B double-checked logo from the 1970s. After the name change to K&B, the double-checked logo was replaced with the new logo. (Author's collection.)

Seen here is the K&B Camera Center envelope after the official name change to K&B. The double-checked logo represented the old drug store, while the new logo took K&B into modern operations that continued to grow. (Author's collection.)

This coupon was included with photographs developed by K&B's photographic processing laboratory. This photograph book can be found today in thousands of homes of customers whose pictures were once developed by K&B. (Author's collection.)

These coupons were included in envelopes holding photographs developed at K&B. In changing its image, K&B's new slogan had become "Personally Yours." K&B stood behind its film developing with a money-back offer if not completely satisfied; no other drug store provided that type of guarantee. (Author's collection.)

Five

COSMETICS COUNTER

"Cosmetics were a big part of our business," says Sydney Besthoff III, once owner of K&B drug stores. In the photographs of the first location on Canal Street, the display cabinets up front are filled with perfumes and lotions of every description. All along the walls are ceiling-high cabinets that clerks retrieved the desired items from. Multiply this by the eventual 186 stores that K&B built, and it is an incredible amount of selection for a drug store. Photographs of the cosmetic counters at different locations throughout the years show expanding cosmetic counters, growing more sophisticated as the times and customers' tastes changed. To paraphrase Sydney Besthoff, "Katz & Besthoff carried a unique inventory." There were perfume lines that K&B exclusively carried in New Orleans, usually embossed with labels or marked brass tops. Also, various creams were inscribed with "Katz & Besthoff New Orleans."

Window displays for ladies' perfumes and men's toiletries were as elaborate as any large department stores. K&B's slogan at the time was "Only the Best," and they lived up to it in everything they displayed and sold. An advertising card from 1924 for Azurea Perfume, a very exclusive perfume that was sold from K&B's cosmetic counter, boasts of four Katz & Besthoff's locations. In the very early days of business, Katz & Besthoff was serious about selling exclusive merchandise to separate them from other local drug stores. In addition to the variety of items carried, K&B always strived to be unique and catered to customers' tastes. Trained beauty consultants were available at each location to assist customers with their selections and offer skin care advice. It was this attention to quality that made K&B drug stores exceptional in their approach to customer service.

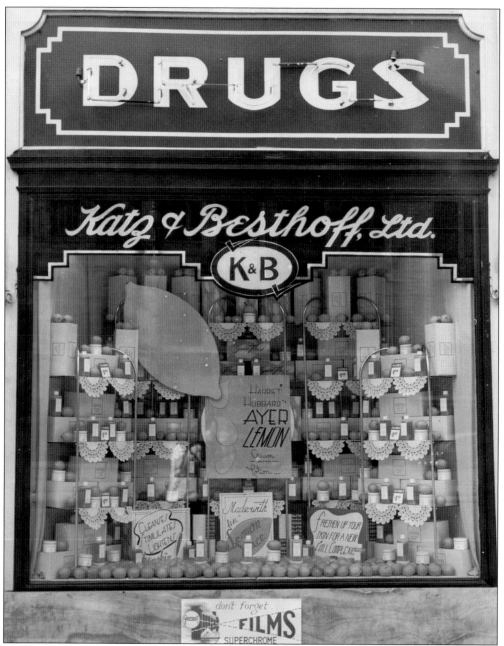

This window display of the Katz & Besthoff at 732 Canal Street from around 1930 advertises Harriet Hubbard Ayer creams and lotions scented with real lemons. K&B took great pride in its products by advertising their exclusivity. (Courtesy Besthoff Family Collection.)

Seen here is an early cold cream jar sold by Katz & Besthoff with the drug store's name and city embossed on the brass top. K&B was very proud of its cosmetic selection and wanted customers to remember where their products had been purchased. (Author's collection.)

This box of Gloria bath powder is from the 1920s. The Katz & Besthoff name and city are embossed on the box's label. Ninety years later, the box still has powder in it. (Author's collection.)

A FRAGRANT SOUVENIR
FROM

KATZ & BESTHOFF, Ltd.

ONLY THE BEST

FOUR STORES

NEW ORLEANS, LA.

L.T. PIVER
PARIS

AZUREA

EXTRACT, FACE POWDER
SACHET POWDER

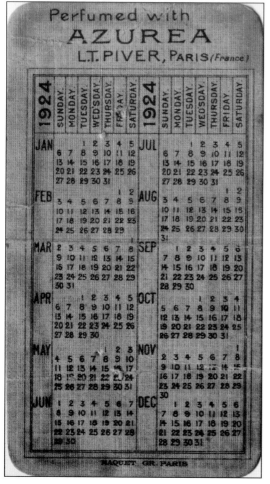

Perfumed with
AZUREA
L.T. PIVER, PARIS (France)

In this image is a scented Azurea perfume sample advert calendar card from 1924 that accompanied the purchase of Azurea perfume from K&B drug store. Note the mention of K&B's four locations. Azurea was a very exclusive perfume sold only in finer department stores, as well as at K&B drug stores. (Author's collection.)

Seen here is the reverse side of the Azurea perfume card displaying a 1924 calendar. The Oak Street and Carrollton Avenue location opened in 1923 and was the fourth K&B drug store since opening in 1905. (Author's collection.)

This is the cosmetics counter at the Oak Street and Carrollton Avenue store. K&B prided itself in offering a diverse and often exclusive selection of cosmetics to men and women. This image was captured in 1962, after the original store, which was built in 1923, had been demolished and this new building was established. The building still stands today as a Rite Aid drug store. (Courtesy Besthoff Family Collection.)

At right is a cosmetics counter at an unknown K&B location in the 1960s. The cosmetics counter offered a variety of makeup and perfumes. K&B's selection equaled, and in some cases surpassed, department store offerings in New Orleans. (Courtesy Besthoff Family Collection.)

Seen here, Katz & Besthoff's 732 Canal Street location is advertising a sale on scented soaps. This K&B had a marble facade with the name tiled into the sidewalk. Note the advertisement stating that Katz & Besthoff are the "sole agents" for Huyler's Candy. Exclusive product selection made K&B unique among competing drug stores in the city. (Courtesy Besthoff Family Collection.)

This is a bottle of Azurea perfume powder that was sold with the scented card pictured here. Azurea perfume was a very exclusive line found only in finer stores, and K&B prided itself on carrying these perfumes in their local drug stores. (Author's collection.)

Six

K&B Brands

Katz & Besthoff–brand items could probably fill a book by themselves. Long before store-brand items became popular or even the norm, Katz & Besthoff had their own brand of almost everything imaginable. Every school kid from New Orleans to Memphis had K&B purple pencils in their backpack at some point during their education. Naturally, with the pencils came the K&B notebook or K&B paper, all in the familiar K&B purple. There was K&B school glue and K&B book covers, though most kids just used K&B bags to make their book covers. The long list of K&B–brand items includes almost everything on the stores' shelves, from cigars to glue. All of it is fondly remembered and tightly held on to if found in a drawer or bathroom cabinet today. The older items have the full K&B double-checked logo with "Only the Best" and "Katz & Besthoff" proudly labeled on them. After the name was officially changed in the late 1970s, the items were just marked with "K&B" in the signature purple color.

Finding an old K&B item or price tag always brings a smile and a story. Anything with a K&B price tag on it is treated like a ticket to the 1939 World's Fair—it is proof that you were really there. Every item has a story behind it, and many are silent reminders of another time that seemed like it would go on forever. The time is quickly approaching when people will find the purple pencils, tablets, cassette tapes, and pens with the initials "K&B" on them and won't know their significance. All of these items sitting around in closets and cabinets will insure that K&B itself will always be around in some form, reminding future generations how much they missed.

K&B had their own brand items long before it was fashionable to market in-house brands. This container of K&B talcum powder dates back to the late 1940s. (Courtesy Besthoff Family Collection.)

Vident dental products were marketed under the Katz & Besthoff brand. The Vident brand included mouthwash, tooth powder, and several other items for dental hygiene. (Courtesy Besthoff Family Collection.)

These shelves are filled with K&B aspirin; Kahol, K&B's own alcohol; KaGel; a K&B antacid; and K&B vitamins. K&B sold a large variety of products under the Katz & Besthoff brand. (Courtesy Besthoff Family Collection.)

Among the floor lamps and kitchen items for sale is the K&B–brand cleaning solution, as seen on the shelves. (Courtesy Besthoff Family Collection.)

The most remembered of all the K&B brands was the ice cream. K&B ice cream was available in 50 flavors, and one of the favorites was Creole Cream Cheese. Note the Jiffy Pop popcorn and the 45 vinyl records. (Courtesy Besthoff Family Collection.)

K&B–brand aspirin fills the shelves at this unknown location. K&B was one of the first drug stores to carry their own name-brand items. (Courtesy Besthoff Family Collection.)

This photograph from the newly remodeled and rebuilt K&B no. 4 shows the selection of candies and liquor along the wall. Some of the liquor was K&B's own brand, which had a following of its own. (Besthoff Family Collection.)

In the days of K&B, every school-age student from first grade to graduate school had used a purple K&B pencil at some point in their life. These can still be found at flea markets, antique malls, and many kitchen drawers in New Orleans today. (Courtesy Besthoff Family Collection.)

K&B sold several brands of cigars but were partial to their own reasonably priced brand. Nothing about the packaging indicated that the K&B brands were anything less than the more expensive ones. (Courtesy Besthoff Family Collection.)

At the time this picture was taken at Katz & Besthoff on 732 Canal Street, the Cremo 5¢ was considered an expensive cigar. Cremo was a Katz & Besthoff in-house brand. (Courtesy Besthoff Family Collection.)

K&B items over the years are seen with this K&B-brand legal pad. The items on the pad are a purple stapler that was used at the checkout, a relief manager's badge, the infamous pen that used purple ink, and dental floss marked with the simple K&B logo. (Author's collection.)

K&B put their logo on everything, even this child's truck from the 1970s. The cab and the lettering on the toy trucks are the perfect shade of K&B purple. (Author's collection.)

In the photograph above, a window display from the K&B no. 5 store on St. Charles Avenue uses several cardboard figures for each advertisement. The liquor displayed is also K&B's own brand. Note the messenger's bike parked on the side of the building that was used for delivering prescriptions to customers. (Courtesy Besthoff Family Collection.)

The shelves in this photograph are stocked with K&B's own brand of plastic wrap and baggies. K&B carried all name-brand items as well as their own brand items, which were less expensive. (Courtesy Besthoff Family Collection.)

Seven

K&B LOCATIONS

Katz & Besthoff evolved from a downtown shopping district drug store established in 1905 at 732 Canal Street to two uptown drug stores and two downtown locations that opened over the next 18 years. Photographs from these years show the progression of the small niche drug stores to single-standing neighborhood buildings, some of the same general design. It is interesting to see the images of advertisements in the K&B windows and the style of the homes in the surrounding neighborhoods of New Orleans in the 1930s and 1940s.

By the 1950s and 1960s, pictures show much more modern building designs for the drug stores, which had moved to the outer suburbs of New Orleans. The drug store anchors of suburban strip shopping centers were larger, with lots of glass, creating an open look in keeping with the architecture of the times. The small neighborhood drug stores were quickly becoming obsolete, with the suburban stores being built to accommodate multiple neighborhoods.

The 1970s and 1980s were decades of shopping malls, so K&B drug stores occupied space in each of the metropolitan area malls. In the early 1970s, every store location had soda fountains and food service, but this was short-lived as all the drug stores discontinued food service in the late 1970s. Clearview Mall was the last metropolitan mall to have a soda fountain in New Orleans; today, the location is occupied by Zea's Restaurant. New drug stores with drive-up prescription windows and redesigned pharmacies were the prototype of the 1990s, which was the last change in K&B's design before it was sold to the Rite Aid group. In all instances, K&B changed with the times, keeping up with the shopping patterns of communities where the drug stores were located. At the time of its sale, K&B had 6 stores in Texas, 20 in Alabama, 103 in Louisiana, 7 in Tennessee, 25 in Mississippi, and 9 in Florida.

This undated photograph shows the first Katz & Besthoff drug store with signs in the windows welcoming Carnival visitors. The pharmacy was originally only on the first floor, with the other floors rented out to other businesses. The sign in the second floor window says "Katz & Besthoff, since 1905, prescription specialists." (Courtesy Besthoff Family Collection.)

The lines superimposed on the photograph above illustrate what the new K&B drug store at Louisiana and St. Charles Avenues would look like. The Ghisalberti building shown was demolished. (Courtesy Besthoff Family Collection.)

KATZ & BESTHOFF STORE NO.
ST. CHARLES & LOUISIANA AVENU

SEIFERTH & GIBERT · ARCHITECT
528 AUDUBON BUILDING   NEW ORLEANS, L

Seen here is an architectural drawing of the new K&B drug store built in 1967 on Louisiana and St. Charles Avenue after the Ghisalberti building was torn down. (Courtesy Besthoff Family Collection.)

In 1967, this K&B drug store replaced the old structure, the demolished Ghisalberti building, which had housed the second K&B location since 1923. The building still stands today, relatively unchanged, as a Rite Aid. (Courtesy Besthoff Family Collection.)

An early morning photograph shows K&B employees stocking the newly built location at St. Charles and Louisiana Avenues before its opening in 1967. The soda fountain can be seen in the rear of the store. (Courtesy Besthoff Family Collection.)

K&B occupied this location on the riverside of Carrollton and Claiborne Avenues until 1959, when they built a new drug store diagonally across the intersection. This location later became Bradley's Restaurant and was eventually torn down. The site has become the home to several banks over the years, but the houses seen behind the drug store still stand today. (Courtesy Besthoff Family Collection.)

This K&B location, built in 1959, replaced the store located diagonally across the street on Carrollton and Claiborne Avenues. A huge clock later occupied the space below the giant sign on the front. The building was abandoned after the sale of K&B to Rite Aid. In 2005, after years of being empty and neglected, the structure was demolished, partially with the help of Hurricane Katrina. Today, a Walgreen's drug store stands on the site (Courtesy Besthoff Family Collection.).

This is a view of the K&B drug store on the corner of Carrollton and Claiborne Avenues. Locals referred to this busy corner as the "center of the universe" because it was the beginning and termination point for several bus and streetcar lines taking people to and from work and school. This K&B location was always full of people, day and night. (Courtesy Besthoff Family Collection.)

In September 1965, Hurricane Betsy hit New Orleans and its suburbs, flooding areas of the city and leaving it without power for weeks. This photograph shows the damage sustained by the K&B drug store at Carrollton and Claiborne Avenues (note the bus in the background). However, it, like all other K&B locations, was open for business. (Courtesy Besthoff Family Collection.)

This image shows the damage to K&B's offices and ice cream-making facility at 900 Camp Street after Hurricane Betsy in September 1965. The downtown area of New Orleans was not hit hard like the suburbs. (Courtesy Besthoff Family Collection.)

This Katz & Besthoff opened in 1950 at 200 Canal Street after K&B's first location at 732 Canal Street was moved. This location was closed in 1974 following relocation to General De Gaulle Avenue in New Orleans. This location was previously the last Liggett drug store in the South. (Courtesy Besthoff Family Collection.)

This photograph from the early 1940s shows a group of people standing outside Katz & Besthoff's fifth location at 7731 St. Charles Avenue in New Orleans. The snapshot was taken in the winter; everyone is wearing a coat or sweater. This is the same location pictured on the cover of this book. (Courtesy Besthoff Family Collection.)

This is a close up of an advertisement announcing the opening of K&B's sixth location at Napoleon and Claiborne Avenues in New Orleans. Note the fountain attendant serving a customer waiting at the curb in his automobile. (Courtesy Todd Norman.)

At right is the full newspaper advertisement from 1929, announcing the opening of the sixth Katz & Besthoff on Napoleon and Claiborne Avenues. Note the sale prices of items at K&B in honor of the new store's opening. (Courtesy Todd Norman)

This is another view of the K&B drug store location at Napoleon and Claiborne Avenue, several years after it first opened in 1929. The original front overhang has been removed, and K&B awnings have been placed on the windows. By this time, curb service was long forgotten. This building was demolished in 1975 and eventually replaced with a new K&B. Today Touro Hospital's Imaging Center occupies the site. (Courtesy Besthoff Family Collection.)

Photographed here is the eighth K&B location at 1320 North Broad Street in New Orleans. The architecture is the same as the fifth store on St. Charles and sixth on Napoleon and South Claiborne Avenues. As populations moved to the suburbs, K&B changed with the times and began changing the looks of their stores. (Courtesy Besthoff Family Collection.)

In 1959, Katz & Besthoff opened the 20th location at 3705 Jefferson Highway in Jefferson Parish, a suburb of New Orleans. The locations were becoming larger with more available parking. This store closed in 1978 and was demolished in 1990. A Wendy's restaurant occupies the site today. (Courtesy Besthoff Family Collection.)

This K&B is located on Metairie Road in Metairie, where, after the war, young couples were building homes. Strip malls were becoming fashionable and needed big-name stores to attract customers. (Courtesy Besthoff Family Collection.)

Seen here is another view of the Metairie Road location after awnings had been added to the outside. (Courtesy Besthoff Family Collection.)

The tenth location was at 4401 St. Charles Avenue. It was rebuilt in 1955 after the original drug store building that opened in 1934 was demolished. This structure was demolished in 2007, and a Capital One Bank stands on the site today. (Courtesy Besthoff Family Collection.)

This is another view of the 4401 St. Charles Avenue location during construction just before it opened. The workman's ladder is still out front alongside a car that will be raffled off in celebration of the reopening of this remodeled location. (Courtesy Besthoff Family Collection.)

The 16th Katz & Besthoff location opened in Gentilly, a suburb of New Orleans, in 1947. During the late 1940s and the 1950s, the drug stores were being built larger and anchored strip malls. (Courtesy Besthoff Family Collection.)

In 1955, Katz & Besthoff celebrated 50 years in business and began raffling off automobiles and appliances to mark the event. This car was displayed outside of the new K&B located in the Carrollton Shopping Center in New Orleans. The crowd is awaiting the winning card to be drawn for the car. (Courtesy Besthoff Family Collection.)

This flyer advertised the prizes while promoting the opening of the newly rebuilt Katz & Besthoff drug store at St. Charles and Napoleon Avenues in 1955. Note the expensive prizes being given away. (Courtesy Besthoff Family Collection.)

This former K&B location in Jefferson, Louisiana, a suburb of New Orleans, was built in 1978. After closing the location at 3750 Jefferson Highway, the building still stands today as a Rite Aid. (Author's collection.)

This is a photograph of the Carrollton Shopping Center, another New Orleans location of Katz & Besthoff drug stores, shortly before its opening in 1955. The facades of the drug stores were K&B purple. (Courtesy Besthoff Family Collection.)

K&B celebrated 50 years in business with an employee banquet held in the grand ballroom of the Roosevelt Hotel in New Orleans. All locations closed at 6 p.m. that day, allowing employees to attend. Standing at the podium in this photograph is Sydney Besthoff Jr., and to his left is Sydney Besthoff III, who oversaw K&B's remarkable growth as chief executive officer. (Courtesy Besthoff Family Collection.)

3940 Canal Boulevard in New Orleans was the home to the eleventh location of Katz & Besthoff. This photograph was taken in 1966. This site, like the older ones, occupied a small niche in an old building. (Courtesy Besthoff Family Collection.)

This former Waterbury's drug store was opened by Katz & Besthoff on Harrison Avenue in Lakeview, a suburb on New Orleans, in 1961. In 1997, this location was moved a few blocks away, closer to Canal Boulevard. In August 2005, this area was under 10 feet of water for several days after a levee broke nearby during Hurricane Katrina. (Courtesy Besthoff Family Collection.)

This photograph from 1961 shows the K&B drug store on Chef Menteur Highway in New Orleans. This location was in eastern New Orleans, once a heavily traveled main thoroughfare to the Mississippi Gulf Coast. (Courtesy Besthoff Family Collection.)

This K&B was on Avenue D in Marrero, Louisiana, a suburb of New Orleans situated across the Mississippi River. The location opened in 1965. During the late 1950s and 1960, new stores were similar in design and size. All of the stores had soda fountains and were anchors for strip malls. This location stands today as a Rite Aid. (Courtesy Besthoff Family Collection.)

Above is a 1966 photograph of the Katz & Besthoff drug store on Veterans Highway in Metairie. Over the next few years, K&B would open several new locations on Veterans Highway. (Courtesy Besthoff Family Collection.)

In this photograph, K&B cigars can be seen in boxes on the tobacco counter at the Veterans and Martin Behrman location in Metairie, which opened in the 1970s. Note the pipe display above the counter and the multitude of tobacco products available. (Courtesy Besthoff Family Collection.)

Built in the late 1970s, this K&B on Veterans Highway and Martin Behrman Avenue in Metairie had stopped using the word "soda" on the front of the building. The soda fountains were being phased out, and drug store fronts reflected the change. At the time, it didn't seem like a big deal, but a few years later customers missed the familiar fountains. (Courtesy Besthoff Family Collection.)

This line of customers is waiting to be checked out at the new K&B location at Veterans Highway and Martin Behrman Avenue in Metairie. The gate marked "in" was present in all the locations and opened as customers walked into the drug store. The only way out of the store was through the checkout line. Walking in to a K&B offered an overwhelming sight of merchandise on every shelf and counter top. (Courtesy Besthoff Family Collection.)

This K&B opened on December 1, 1966, on Jefferson Highway in Harahan, Louisiana, a suburb of New Orleans. There was a full-service soda fountain at this location. This K&B was relocated a few miles from this site in 1997. The building still stands today as a Dollar General store. (Courtesy Besthoff Family Collection.)

This photograph provides a closer look at the K&B drug store in Harahan, Louisiana, which opened in early December 1966. Note the Santa Claus sign on the roof inviting people to buy at K&B. This K&B location was the anchor store for this shopping center. (Courtesy Besthoff Family Collection.)

This is a photograph of the K&B drug store located at 5201 Canal Boulevard in New Orleans after it was rebuilt in 1976. The original building that was there since 1946 was demolished and replaced with this new building, which still stands today. (Courtesy Besthoff Family Collection.)

Above is the former K&B in Harahan, Louisiana, which originally opened in 1966, as it looks today. The windows have been bricked over and the parking lot has been rearranged. (Author's collection.)

Above is an architectural drawing of K&B store no. 28 built in 1965 at 7201 St. Claude Avenue. Note that the word "soda" is still used on the front. This was before the soda fountains were discontinued in the stores. (Courtesy Besthoff Family Collection.)

The Harahan, Louisiana, location opened in 1978 after moving from its former location that had opened in 1966. Rite Aid added a drive-through to this location after the purchase of K&B. (Author's collection.)

The K&B Kenilworth Shopping Center location in eastern New Orleans is captured in this 1970 photograph. The architecture is still changing, and the soda fountains have been discontinued with the removal of the word "soda" from the sign on the building. (Courtesy Besthoff Family Collection.)

After Hurricane Camille hit the Gulf Coast in 1969, this K&B in St. Bernard, Louisiana, south of New Orleans, sustained water and wind damage. The cars have been parked close to the building to avoid being flooded. (Courtesy Besthoff Family Collection.)

This is a closer look at the K&B in St. Bernard, Louisiana. In addition to the water damage, one of the store windows has been blown in. (Courtesy Besthoff Family Collection.)

In 1965, Hurricane Betsy hit New Orleans and its surrounding suburbs. This K&B location was on Metairie Road. The windows were blown in and the store was flooded. (Courtesy Besthoff Family Collection.)

Seen here is a look inside the K&B Metairie Road location after Hurricane Betsy blew the windows in. Several K&B locations were damaged by the storm, but they returned to service as quickly as possible. There were no Wal-Marts in New Orleans in 1965—K&B was the closest thing to it. (Courtesy Besthoff Family Collection.)

This is the K&B at Carrollton Shopping Center in New Orleans after Hurricane Betsy. The store opened for business after the storm had passed. The windows are still taped to prevent them from shattering during the storm. The suburbs of New Orleans suffered more damage than areas close to city, like where this K&B was located. (Courtesy Besthoff Family Collection.)

The Oakwood Shopping Center Mall K&B location opened in 1970. K&B mall locations were usually self-standing structures with an outside, as well as an inside entrance, to the mall. (Courtesy Besthoff Family Collection.)

This was the K&B on General De Gaulle Avenue in New Orleans. After the closing of K&B at 200 St. Charles Avenue, this location was given the designation of store no. 1. (Courtesy Besthoff Family Collection.)

Read Road in New Orleans East is the location of this K&B, which was built in 1977. The architecture had changed from the little neighborhood drug stores into a much larger scale. With no soda fountains, K&B was able to increase their retail space for customers. (Courtesy Besthoff Family Collection.)

Outside the 900 Camp Street offices and warehouse, a delivery truck is waiting to be loaded. Note the help wanted sign on the building, directing people to the second floor. This photograph was taken in the late 1940s. (Courtesy Besthoff Family Collection.)

The 1011 Canal Street Katz & Besthoff location, which opened in 1937, advertises Gillette razors with a small sign in the window regarding the World Series on WNOE radio. This location was K&B's 12th. It closed in 1962. (Courtesy Besthoff Family Collection.)

The K&B Plaza at 1055 St. Charles Avenue was purchased by K&B in 1974. This was the headquarters of K&B drug stores until its closing in 1997. One huge K&B sign remains on the top of the building facing St Charles Avenue, reminding passing commuters of better days. (Courtesy Besthoff Family Collection.)

Eight

K&B Closes, 1997

Time is marked in New Orleans by anniversaries of births, deaths, hurricanes, and the closing of K&B drug stores. The common themes among all of those events are that they changed people's lives, and the closing of K&B drug stores is no exception. Soon after K&B's closing, Rite Aid had a tent sale for K&B items outside one of the old locations on a rainy Saturday morning. In any other city, the event would have passed unnoticed, but not in New Orleans. The tent sale was packed with people, buying anything purple with the K&B logo on it to remember a place that had been a part of their lives. K&B's sale left behind a huge debris field, much like after the sinking of a great ship. Purple bags, pens, matches, patches, and service pins keep the "purple dragon" in our memories.

Some will remember stopping at the K&B on the corner of Carrollton and Claiborne Avenues on the way to and from high school, the soda fountain with the little jukeboxes at each table, or the freshly baked biscuits served for breakfast every morning. The corner has been referred to as "the center of the universe," and it certainly was for years for many people as they headed to a Tulane University football game at Tulane Stadium on Saturday afternoons or to watch the New Orleans Saints play on Sunday afternoons. Standing on St. Charles Avenue, waiting for the parades to pass, looking around on almost every corner—a K&B drug store could be found. It was the central meeting place for most crowd gatherings, especially during Mardi Gras. Christmas, Easter, Halloween, and New Years Eve usually meant going to K&B at some point during the day. Viewing old photographs of the K&B locations brings the drug store back for just a little while, creating a pleasant interlude of memories.

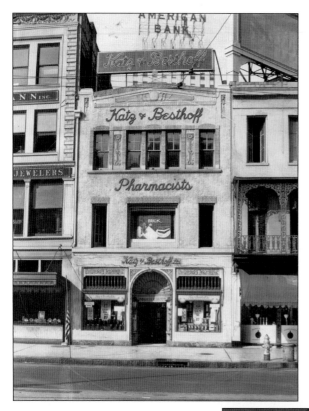

It all started in a small drug store in 1905. This photograph was taken during the 1930s. The drug store had changed its storefront several times over 25 years. Note the Orange Julius stand in the store next door to the right. (Courtesy Besthoff Family Collection.)

Sydney Besthoff III (left) shakes hands with his father Sydney Besthoff Jr. (right) under the photograph of Sydney Besthoff Sr., who cofounded the Katz & Besthoff drug store in 1905 with fellow pharmacist Gustave Katz. (Courtesy Besthoff Family Collection.)

Seen above, a Katz & Besthoff delivery truck is parked in front of the newly opened 841 Canal Street store in 1911. The photograph shows the building being renovated shortly after its purchase. The man seated out front is most likely the architect. Note the full wheelbarrow just behind the delivery truck. This was across the street from the Maison Blanche department store. (Courtesy Besthoff Family Collection.)

K&B drug stores stopped delivery services in the late 1950s as a result of escalating liability costs. Medications and ice cream had been delivered to customers' homes since K&B's beginning in 1905. (Courtesy Besthoff Family Collection.)

In this 1920s photograph, an elaborate window display at Katz & Besthoff's 732 Canal Street drug store advertises the new Gillette One Piece Razors for men. Window displays were the most important type of advertising in downtown New Orleans on Canal Street. (Courtesy Besthoff Family Collection.)

Edward. L. Chapotel, Katz & Besthoff general manager, holds a sales meeting on the fourth floor of K&B's drug store at 1011 Canal Street. E.L. Chapotel was the manager of Katz & Besthoff's second drug store that opened in 1911. He later became vice president and general manager of all K&B stores. The 1011 Canal Street store closed in 1962. (Courtesy Besthoff Family Collection.)

Sales were clearly important at K&B, and employees were actively involved in programs to increase business. This photograph shows a sales display promotion from 1942 featuring a drawing of S.J. Besthoff Jr. in a helmet, leading the battle to increase sales. (Courtesy Besthoff Family Collection.)

War bonds are the focus of this window display at Katz & Besthoff's 732 Canal Street drug store. S.J. Besthoff Jr. was serving in the Army during World War II, and each K&B drug store was no less patriotic. (Courtesy Besthoff Family Collection.)

A huge advertisement for war bonds stands behind Katz & Besthoff's store no. 6 on Claiborne and Napoleon Avenues. Note the small sign on the sidewalk announcing no curb service. (Courtesy Besthoff Family Collection.)

Here, K&B celebrates its 50th anniversary in the grand ballroom of the Roosevelt Hotel. By this time, the Besthoff family had become sole owners of the Katz & Besthoff drug stores. Gustave Katz had died in 1940, and his family sold their interests in the store. The second and third generation of the Besthoff family had begun to increase locations and sales that would make the drug store chain a multistate operation. (Courtesy Besthoff Family Collection.)

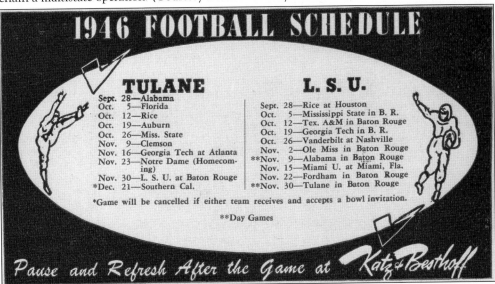

Katz & Besthoff distributed this 1946 football schedule in the hopes of keeping their soda fountain in customers' thoughts during football season. (Courtesy Besthoff Family Collection.)

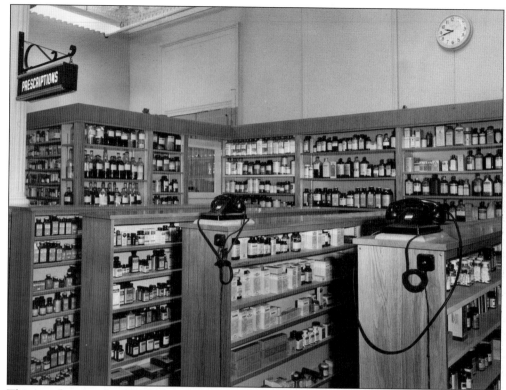

This is a photograph of K&B drug store no. 9 at 235 Carondelet Street in New Orleans showing a well-stocked pharmacy with multiple telephones. (Courtesy Besthoff Family Collection.)

Purple aisle markers indicate the various items located throughout the drug store, as illustrated in this photograph from the 1970s. Customers of K&B know the familiar feeling of walking into the drug store and having no doubt that they will find whatever it is they are looking for. (Courtesy Besthoff Family Collection.)

The ice cream case greeted customers as they walked in to the store, and it was also their last stop as they walked out. K&B ice cream is still talked about fondly, even though the stores closed over a decade ago. (Courtesy Besthoff Family Collection.)

Sydney Besthoff III (second from left) cuts the ribbon opening K&B's first out-of-town store in Slidell, Louisiana, a suburb 20 miles outside the city. (Courtesy Besthoff Family Collection.)

The next out-of-town K&B location was in Sulphur, Louisiana, west of New Orleans. Sydney Besthoff III (wearing a ribbon on his coat) opens the store. Standing at the far left is James Leblanc, president and chief operating officer of K&B drug stores. Besthoff and Leblanc were the driving forces that expanded K&B to a total of 186 stores by 1997. (Courtesy Besthoff Family Collection.)

James Leblanc, president and chief operating officer of K&B drug stores (right) stands with Jac Stich (center) and Charles Stich (left). The Stiches were Besthoff family cousins who ran K&B during the war years while S.J. Besthoff Jr. served in the Army. All of these men were devoted to Katz & Besthoff drug stores, and their management made it the retail giant it eventually became known as. (Courtesy Besthoff Family Collection.)

Seen here are several different uniform patches worn by K&B pharmacists and managers during the last few years of the drug store. These were also worn on the infamous purple vests worn by store managers. (Author's collection.)

Comparing this image of display cases used in the later drug stores with the photographs of the cases used in the first Katz & Besthoff at 732 Canal Street proves how much the stores changed in style but stayed the same in sales philosophy. (Courtesy Besthoff Family Collection.)

K&B's greeting card aisle would usually be filled with customers searching for the right one during various holidays. K&B's card selection, like everything else in the store, was larger than other drug stores. (Courtesy Besthoff Family Collection.)

The *K&B Connection*

Vol. 8 No. 1   FINAL EDITION   September, 1997

Personally Yours...

A History of K&B

*In 1994, Sandie Gauthreaux wrote "The History of K&B" for a class she was taking at Our Lady of Holy Cross College in New Orleans. We published it in three different editions of **The K&B Connection** for you in 1995, our 90th anniversary year. We thought you would like to have the complete history in this, our final edition.*

"Want a partner?" asked Gus Katz. "Yes," answered Syd Besthoff, "if I could find one like yourself." "You've got one. When do we start?" This casual conversation took place in the drugstore of Gustave Katz, at St. Charles and Jackson Avenues. It marked the beginning of the native New Orleanian drugstore chain named Katz and Besthoff, Ltd., more commonly known today as K&B.

Our founders

he owned a prospering drugstore business. His wife was the former Miss Florence Stich of New Orleans. When he had come here to be married, he briefly met Mr. Katz. The two men discussed the business. In April of 1905, Besthoff returned here because Mrs. Besthoff's parents were anxious to have their daughter and young grandson close to them. Mr. Besthoff dropped in at the uptown store of Gus Katz. He had already decided that Canal Street would meet his ambitions for the site of his new drugstore. With the brief conversation between Besthoff and Katz, a business partnership was formed that would prosper and endure many hardships through the years.

This partnership began immediately. Katz sold his St. Charles Avenue store and the new firm of Katz and Besthoff, Ltd., was opened at 732 Canal Street. Many prior drugstores on Canal Street had failed but not Katz and Besthoff. In the heart of the shopping district, they adopted the slogan, "Only the best." The store's success can be greatly attributed to the two owners' complementing personalities, as

Secretary/Treasurer. Maurice Stich and Frederick Katz were also members of the Board. Certificates of stock were issued and signed by Sydney J. Besthoff and Gustave Katz. Besthoff and Katz were given 144 shares each and Stich and F. Katz were sold one share each. All shareholders agreed not to part with or dispose of any stock they owned without first offering it to the other directors and stockholders. The contents of the Katz store were bought by the new firm. It was agreed that all checks, drafts, bills of exchange, promissory notes, and other commercial papers, acts and agreements

Katz & Besthoff, Ltd.
1910 Logo

of the company would be signed by the President or Secretary/Treasurer. The salaries of both the President and Secretary/Treasurer were set at

The *K&B Connection* for September 1997 published the history of K&B with photographs of the original location at 732 Canal Street and the company founders, Gustave Katz and Sydney Besthoff. The newspaper's final article was written by the company's president, James LeBlanc. (Courtesy Besthoff Family Collection.)

This mug was given out to employees at the closing of K&B drug stores. The message on the front sums up the philosophy of K&B, which largely contributed to its success. Employees were treated as friends. To paraphrase a longtime K&B employee, "K&B treated you like a human being." (Courtesy Besthoff Family Collection.)

Sydney Besthoff III is a man who always looks forward to the next challenge. This image was captured in the 1970s in front of the K&B Plaza on St. Charles Avenue in New Orleans. The sculpture Besthoff is posing next to is called *Mississippi*, and it stands in front of the building today. The photograph's edges got wet when Besthoff's home flooded after Hurricane Katrina. (Courtesy Besthoff Family Collection.)

BIBLIOGRAPHY

Besthoff, Sydney J. III. Interview, October 1, 2010.

Frederick, James. "Jim Leblanc: K&B Services; president and chief operating officer." *Drug Store News*. May 20, 1996.

Gautreaux, Sandie. "A History of K&B." *The K&B Connection 8.1*. September 1997.

Jumonville, Florence. "Purple Passion: Ephemera from K&B Drugstores." *Ephemera News* vol. 3, Spring 2004.

Leblanc, James. "The End or the Beginning?" *The K&B Connection 8.1*. September 1997.

Symons, Allene. "New Prototype, renovations overtake traditions at K&B." *Drug Store News* March 2, 1992.

DISCOVER THOUSANDS OF LOCAL HISTORY BOOKS
FEATURING MILLIONS OF VINTAGE IMAGES

Arcadia Publishing, the leading local history publisher in the United States, is committed to making history accessible and meaningful through publishing books that celebrate and preserve the heritage of America's people and places.

Find more books like this at
www.arcadiapublishing.com

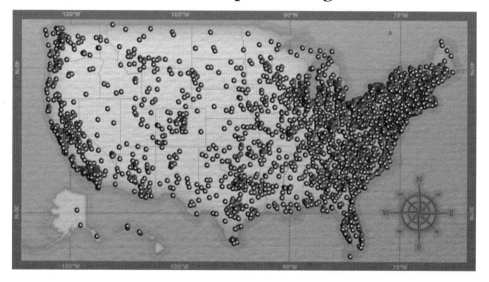

Search for your hometown history, your old stomping grounds, and even your favorite sports team.